# A Legacy of

# Timeless

# Wisdom

**E. Pat Fulwood-White**

Williams and King Publishers
Orlando, Florida
ISBN: 9780998366333

Printed in the USA

# PREFACE

This book is a compilation of poetry, thoughts, and quotations of E. Pat Fulwood-White. Throughout many years, she has dedicated herself to composing and sharing with readers, a window of her life's experiences and her gifts in words and poetry. This literary work is divided into two sections: Inspirational Thoughts and Poems.

# Table of Contents

# A Legacy of

# Timeless

# Wisdom

# Inspirational Thoughts

**01.03.70**

Know that love has no labels…just truth.

**03.14.70**

## Smile

Know that when you learn that
your mission
is to live the best life you can.
Your life.
Not the life of someone else.
Embrace and build your dignity.
Smile!

**12.24.73**

Why do women give up so much of
themselves to walk in sync with
someone else's destiny instead of
following their own blueprints?

**02.18.75**

When I prayed, He smiled.

**02.18.75**

When you truly learn that there is absolutely
nothing between you and God
Not one thing.
Not even a breath.
No, not one.


Know that an examination may reveal to the
world what caused your death,
But cannot tell the world how
intense you have
loved or lived.


**02.24.75**

## *Know*

Know your destiny is cemented in
the woven threads of time.


**03.15.75**

The moment I believed,
my soul felt at peace

**08.23.75**

Your (our) quality of life is what
you have etched
in your soul.
It will create a vision for your
goals in life.

**02.24.76**

## *Love*

As the sun chased the night from the earth,
The blue-silver shade of the dawn rises
to the peek over the edge of the universe saying,
"Hello world."
Life is showing us a new and unseen beautiful day.

**09.25.80**

Let's satisfy our appetite for knowledge
with thirst for a great education.

**03.21.82**

We must get to a point where we
know when the game is won.
Losing is not always a bad thing.
The lesson is just different.

**01.03.83**

# *Victory*

Victory goes to the player who is
able to endure the challenge.

**02.18.83**

Know that our distractions take place
when our goals are put on hold.

**12.24.83**

# *Love (2)*

I'm free and easy.
Life is just that way.

**02.14.84**

## *This Day*

On this day as I saw you,
My heart opened up like a window to the
joy of an evening's sunset.
I then, will raise my eyes to the sky alone.
Opening my mind and soul to the inner
peace and love which awaits me.
On this day when we will love with
the gift of togetherness
that transcends the destiny of time.

**01.15.85**

Oh, why do we often have an
argument with reality?
Who wins?

**02.07.85**

Know that one must pack and move
and truly leave to come back.
Don't live in the "stay mode"
because you'll never learn how sweet
your own freedom is.

**02.18.85**

He who holds the existence
of your heart must truly have a key to
unlock your destiny.
Do you know whom that might be?

**03.21.85**

Life is a great gift that takes work.
Know that we are considered to be
the "walk-away" society.
Remember God has given us the
night to rest,
so our ability to labor in the vineyard
is refueled by the morning.

**04.29.85**

## Know

Know that I've learned how to be
patient and truly say more than
people will ever need to hear.
There is an unspoken message.
The silence.
In our presence.
In our wisdom.

**05.30.85**

When I can't see where to place my feet,
When I can't feel where to place my hands,
I exhale and move by faith.

**09.25.85**

## *Family*

We all are one
Me in you and you in me.
Then knowing that we are a
collection of us.
A family.
We are connected.

**12.24.85**

Married people don't often communicate.
They took the course that taught them how to
silently tolerate each other's imperfections.
Ahh.

**04.29.86**

Love is transferred through the smile in your voice.
Let others hear that smile when you speak.

**01.12.87**

Mama said, 'When and where do
you exhibit the fullest expression
of your own existence?"
When?
Where?
How?
Lord, I'm not looking back.
I'm done with that.
I'm living solely for your kingdom.
Yes, it is ahead
Above safe where we are wholly fed.

**06.16.88**

# *Maybe*

Maybe it happened because the wind moves
so softly through the trees.
Maybe it happened because the evening sun
captures our breath against the sky.
Maybe it happened because the water moves so
soothing around the edge of the cliff.
Just maybe because loving is a part of living and
living brings forth love.
It happened while walking with confidence which
made a sense of pride show through.
Maybe it happened so I would share it
Happens to you, with you, maybe.

**09.10.88**

Remember to always teach and
encourage your youth.

**02.08.89**

My tolerance has given me the gift to
eliminate, tolerate, and compensate
for the negative forces
that can ruin most relationships.

**06.20.89**

## *Cannot*

You cannot share experiences with
someone you don't love.
You cannot share a smile with those
who can't respect your existence.
You cannot enjoy love with
someone you don't understand.

**07.11.89**

Falling in love is like hitching a
ride on a shooting star.
Moving free, feeling high, learning
and yearning for the unknown.

**08.02.89**

# *A Charm*

Our love has captured a shine, a
sparkle, a spirit and an essence of
lasting chance that is ours forever.

**10.24.89**

One of the greatest sins is keeping
someone's heart
under lock and key knowing that it
will only be
casted aside for the taste of
another.

**01.10.90**

When our heart finds its kindred spirit,
Our soul is made whole.

**02.18.90**

He has the power to calm,
comfort and fix your heart.
Trust Him.  He knows.

**03.21.90**

Know that self-examination
is a bitter pill to swallow,
especially when our Ph.D. is in
judging others.


I've found the love that I wanted
others to give.
I found it in "I-Am."


**08.27.90**

Yes, go on and give up.
Then you will truly feel what pitiful
looks like.
Keep the mirror near,
You will see You.


**12.29.92**

## *Connected*

If you're in the world somewhere,
I can handle where I am.
For your essence is in my soul
I'm you and you are me.

Thoughts of Mama (1924-96)

**06.05.98**

Know that God has put sin on credit.
So, work hard to pay that debt.

**08.25.98**

Dare to be remarkable by exhibiting great
scholarly qualities.

**04.29.99**

## *Forgiveness*

Know that we don't have to like or
love the people who need our
forgiveness.
Just be big enough to free
yourself of the burden and forgive.

**11.27.99**

Present your secret weapon to the world,
Let them see the God you serve in
your daily walk.

**01.12.00**

One of a woman's greatest sacrifices
is to give all that she has for the
growth and care of her children.
Because what she does for the least
of these pleases HIM.

**12.24.99**

Why do we tell others that we are
waiting for God?
Knowing full well it is God who
waits patiently for us.

**12.24.00**

## *Sometimes*

Sometimes I wish that you could see you
through my eyes.
For I look from the windows of my soul.
All the time
Is my sometimes.

**09.30.03**

Let your action be a deposit on
your own journey home.
Remember, this is a "show-me" society.
Yes, what you do is clearer than
what you say.
Let your words and actions present
you to others.

**03.12.04**

# *What a Wonder*

Have you ever wondered why when you rush to catch your
shadow it runs away?
But when you walk away,
it peacefully follows or walks along too?
What a mystery?
What a wonder?

**01.23.05**

Know that you won't ever be in a place where God
can't bend down and help you up.

**02.14.05**

Why do we train ourselves to see only what we want?
Why?

**04.29.06**

The determination to be productive outweighs the need
to be a part of someone's visions.

**04.29.06**

Remain your own person. Stay
grounded in your faith.

**05.30.06**

A mother's love is sweet like the
warmth from the sun.
A mother's love is everlasting and
felt by all who sees her.

**02.08.07**

Inside our souls are housed love, beauty,
empathy, power, and wisdom.
Release it and give to the universe,
The greatness that makes you, you.

**06.31.07**

# *Interruption*

I'm your interruption,
to show you the game.
How long will it take you to make
the last move?
If you choose not to move,
it doesn't mean the game is over.
Work with all
But be labelled by none.

**08.17.07**

Know that our attitude is a huge
part of our character
Have you checked your attitude lately?
Wow!
Let's fall in love again and again.

**08.21.07**

It's a sad thing to be around men
who are intimidated
by successful, confident, and
productive women.

**07.04.08**

Know that a half truth is truly a "whole lie."
So, remembering to bend the truth
doesn't change that lie.

**06.05.09**

Mercy is what we should share with others
and we will receive happiness through giving it.

**06.09.09**

Today I listened to the melody playing in
my heart.
Just a soft melody soothing my soul.

**07.04.10**

When your touch can last until the midnight,
Exchange space with the dawn.
Bask in its beauty and smile.

**09.14.11**

Why do we always say we are waiting for the Lord,
knowing full well it's definitely the other way around.

**04.29.13**

I have come to realize that my
beauty comes from
the light of the Son.
"My life is worth living" is just
only to say,
"Thank you Jesus!"

**03.18.14**

Already, but not yet,
Is how we live our lives
because our faith is still in the
doubting stage.

**02.18.15**

Let's learn to listen to the silence,
And truly witness
the voice of wisdom that speaks to
our soul.

**04.20.15**

We have learned to live by our
conditioned mind.
How sad, because it blocks our
potential to be productive.

## 08.30.15

Let your light shine from the inside and know
that the darkness cannot dim its glow.

## 01.15.16

Let's learn how to make space for
what's important in your day.

You can't stop an idea or a
dream from surfacing.
When the time comes, they will
be unleashed.

## Silence

Stay humble at all cost.
Learn that wisdom grows in silence.

## Then

Comes your face,
Just dancing in my mind.
Playing a tune that attracts my heart
free and easy.
I'm loved.

## Look

Here, it comes like the slow walk a bride takes
Toward her new life and the experience she will
endure with her husband
Setting a pace that will dominate their lives.
Her life, look.

# Daylight

When the daylight dances across the river of time,
We see our souls open to the mighty presence of thee.

# See

When he sets and turns his back, drops his head
The night slowly creeps upon us again
His back blocks the light that will let the darkness in
on the horizon as the world continues to turn.
You say, "sunrise."
We say, "see the beauty of eternity."
You say, "hurry to the field."
We say, "work hard and fast."
We say, "work smart, never hard."
You say, "keep moving, don't waste any time."
We say, "savor every moment,
Feel the awesomeness of our Creator's wisdom".

E. Pat White

# Gran-Mama's Love

My Gran-Mama's love feels like a hug
When mama says "no, just go play".
Mama's not mad child, she just has so much to do.

Gran-Mama's love feels like her soft sweater
that she lays around my shoulders
When I reach up for mama and she rushes
Pass on her way to solve another case.

Gran-Mama's love tastes like cloves she places
on my tongue to soothe my feelings
As I watch mama disappear down the lane
For she has beans to pick and cotton to chop
No distractions. Just work to do.

Gran-Mama's love
Reads to us in the evening
As story made up about the moon,
Telling us that one of you will see
This same moon from someplace else, soon.

Oh, Grandma was so right!
As I traveled the world - only to look up in China
To see that same moon.
Aah, What a beauty! The fullness of its shape
was the same as I remembered as a child,
Sitting beside my Gran-Mama on our porch.

As my travels took me to Brazil
On the cool beach of warm blue hues of the water,

See, look out, look up.

Know that God made billions of stars.
But one Son.
This sun.
One moon.
Its twin.
They reflect each other as we are
Replicas of "Him"
Made in His image.

Gran-Mama said, "Do you know who the twins are?
Sun and Moon."

Like Linda and Leon, like Clara and Ray.
Connected to this day
Yes, their jobs are to complete the other
Caring for each other like a friend
And mothers.

Life is funny like that but challenging and full of surprises.
Enjoy them all.
This farm is big now,
but the places you will go and see are bigger.
Find your way, look back just a little but don't tarry.
Make us proud and travel far.

Send back your smile in your face and voice
Letting Gran-Mama know you're not afraid or lost.
Yes, Gran-Mama's love feels like heaven
And mama's like the clouds,
Being part of them has made me so whole and proud.

*E. Pat White*

# *Poems*

*E. Pat White*

# Mama Knows

Mama has always known she has the connection to our
heart and soul.
She watches out the window as she passes off the meal
She listens to our hearts as the clock ticks away the hour
Knowing the next could be our power
God, she's strong!

Never reaching in the emptiness of the empty space
Connecting to our ancestry that builds a place of trust.
She feeds, she gives, and she matured and led,
Filling our courageous souls with fuel of our destiny.
She walked the halls and prayed for the world
So, when we returned we'd have faith to hold.
Yes, listening, looking, sharing what she
learned from walking in – worthiness.

Songs of praise always on her lips,
Meditation and praise in her heart.
Yes, mama has always known she has
the connection to our hearts and souls.
Our lives are a symphony of her songs
Music that impart beauty and grace,
Covered with faith and mercy from her soul.

Yes, mama knows,
So we worked hard,
Gave our best - all covered with her guidance
and blanketed in her undying love.
Yes! Mama knows.

# *The Fourth-Born*

I was born into a family of eleven awesome souls
The fourth of the clan with great change and quite bold.
We are brought in this universe alone
But already covered in love,
Our journey is prepared to walk destiny's road
As we create the illusion that
our blueprint is set into motion by us.

Yes, the fourth born
Filled with energy and focus
Truly very smart living at ease because of a pure heart,
Answering to her call and place where she falls
Listening with baited breath should mama call.
Never late, never weary, never harsh or stressed
Always prepared and will often do the most.
Dancing to the symphony played from the angelic choir
Humming the songs of ancestry with those from above
Knowing the cost was only true love.

Fourth-born, limitless, pure and free
So easy to be included with grace and shall be.
Just daddy's little girl
Yes, can't you see?
Being watched as she grows,
Dancing, singing all day,
Look at one, two, and three
We all know can only be in order
if you add or see four.

"Born to be a blessing"
My grand-mama would say.

We look to her for wisdom to this very day.

Born with a veil,
See the shadow on her face
All knowing and feeling things from another place.
Enjoy her insight, faith and love
It can only connect the place of peace.

Know there are no limitations
Unless you create them yourself.
Remember your spirit will meet others
It matters because it's you.
Find your balance
Be creative, nurturing, giving and caring
Fourth Born, stay true.

# Walk with Me

Walk with me now girl
Just walk with me.
Why? Why? Why so angry?
Why so mean?
Why so combative about life you haven't seen?
Mama sometimes does know best.
Take a breath and take back your peace.

Just stop and think as the madness is truly released.
Now look in this "ole" piece of glass and tell me what you see.
The face of one "Angel" looking back at me.
Dry those tears and be for real
Can it be all that bad to do what was ask of you?
Why so sad, so "unfair?"
It will be over soon and you will be gone away
To make your own schedule of how your day will play.
So don't be so quick to close your ears
to Mama's wisdom and love,
Because Mama's voice won't sound so demanding
or slick when she speaks to you from above.
She knows your desires, your wants, and your cares.
She stays connected to your wishes and fears.

Your departing is a battle she must fight on her own,
For when you go
she will release you to the light all alone.
Showing her hurt which looks like wrath,
But know it's her love in the aftermath.
We reared you girls like queens on the Nile.
Courageous, faithfulness, witty and with style.

So, stretch out your arms
and give back some of your best love,
For all mothers hurt when a soul leaves the nest.

Now walk with me on this path as we often do
For dad's love is a secret and sometimes yours will be, too.
Can't show that love is our strength and our
weakness, too.
I learn to listen, to love.
You will find it in people who truly care for you.
Now you see,
Just hush and walk with me
Brothers been out here and so has Lean
Learning about life
Wanting to be seen.

I told Eddie, Bear, and Greg that we all have been
hatched from our mama's eggs.
You girls are trying and sometimes
your heads are hard.
But Mama's ways will pave the way.
Linda, Jen, Cynthia, Angie and Poo are all the same
Like Peanut, must learn life's games.
Walk with me child.
Just breathe and calm down.
Know that these lessons
are your true test to keep you around.

# Love, Life, Unity

I waited for your breath.
Waited and waited for fear if I exhaled
I would vanish from deep within my soul.
Waiting as the pain became unbearable,
So unbearable, unbearable
To feel a sense of loss
Not seeing,
Not knowing,
Not having.
Not sharing my existence like the love one I dreamed,
My mirrored twin.

Know that love is our life support.
I went into myself, no air to breathe
I could not find my way out of myself without
you.
Where was my breath?
My exhale would loose me into myself, calling.
Can't you feel my pain in your silence?
Do you know why our hearts hurt?
When there is a pain there, it won't let you be
It hurts because I'm trying to hold the love
inside.

Love can't be contained
It is God, it is boundless
It belongs to the universe.
Love is all around us
in that quiet place.
We all cry sometimes
In that quiet place seeking love.

The legacy of love comes from the heart,
the fiber of our existence.

Challenge your soul
Let it sing to what it feels.
Hold your heart in protective solitude
Guard it with your love.
Purge and go forth,
Sing uncaged.
Sing unconditionally.
Sing to share
Sing to love
Sing for freedom
Just sing, just sing,
Love, Live, Unite!

# Shattered

Hearts are sometimes shattered like pieces of glass
Not able to forget the hurts of the past.
Only to feel the loneliness so much
God how I'd give to be included in a group,
Being apart like the vessels of a fleet.
I've lived the same dream many a night
Hoping for the answers I wanted but being awaken
With a fright that cripples.

I believe memories are the glue greatest of all
Using love as a buffer to break over all.
Love is forever and we all have its strength.
For forever is a long time which can't be measured by us.
So, to love just teaches us to trust
and stay open to what loving truly means.
Somewhere to truly share our hearts for protection.
Shattered, but not totally broken.

# *Shh! Shh!*

Shh!
The door closes softly
As he ushers in the daybreak
He's been gone for days
As my heart aches
He tips back in your lives as if he never left
Picking up where he left off
As if that's how it should be.
No questions.
No answers.
No future.
Little past.

Nothing of use to hold me here
Heart of stone waiting to crack
so brittle and worn.
An entry in your space like that of a cat
creeping and crawling.

Not knowing what to do.
Should I leave?
Should I stay?
Or as he strays,
I stray, too.

Why not walk into your existence
With a pride so bold?
He does not hold the blueprint
to your destiny, I'm told.
Just a chess piece to move
As you set it in its place.

No, not your destiny

He can't change a line
Because it was already set by the Divine.

Shh!
Listen to the quietness
that can't scream so loud.
Your smile in the dark
still makes you proud.
Why creep?
Why hide?
Why diminish your existence?
Walk away while you can
Because leaving is not a cure
Just a plan.
Shh!
Shh!
Shh!
There is no secret
God always knows.
Shh!

# Rev's Love

One of the sweetest things I've ever known
Is praying with Rev. Higgins over the phone.
Hoping others could see her face
As she asks the Lord just to share His grace!
She spoke to Him like a precious floating cloud
So soft, sincere a whisper that can go on for miles.
I know He smiles each time and says,
"That's my child."

I'm proud when the morning comes
And I see the play of the light.
I know God walks, shares
and created His love with all His might,
Giving us time to live and learn.

He'll be there when our bells begin to ring.
I feel that He is truly my shepherd
And I can't go astray.
For He guides my feet day by day
I feel Him in the summer breeze
Wake Him up with my prayers
if you please.

He carries my burdens and never gets tired
Which should keep my soul wholly ghost wired.
Just to tell the story of what is in store for you.

See a piece of His love just for me
That's why the sweetest things
one can behold
Is to listen to Rev. Higgins pray to
God to Strengthen your soul.

*E. Pat White*

# Gutter Girl

Gutter Girl you are so fly
Moving around without a care
Letting your life pass you by.

Looking for fun
Going to and fro
Running up and down from door to door.
No one cares how smart you are
Just giving up your youth to ride in the car.
Girl please, slow yourself down
Let the air ride in your peace
Just stay cool down and enjoy the moment
Relent, breathe, relax, choose.

Stop stirring up trouble causing a fuss.
You know your decisions have consequences,
they must.
So, slow your roll so you can build up some trust
Found in the best of us
With your speed the wind gets cracked,
Confused not knowing how to move
As it dances around your face with focus and ease.

Gutter girl you truly are fly
But will you know what not to try?
You are giving directions telling all which way to go
Not realizing the garbage you have in tow.
Holding that finger over your head
calling out names of the past you see.
Showing the new bred that loving protects me.

Gutter Girl you are a bad-ass you think,
Rushing your existence,

Following all those winks.
Thinking they are true sincere and pure
Forgetting to pay attention to where it came from.

Keep up the pace and let the wind pass by
use its force to help you glide,
For the trouble you meet
Looks like fun on the beat,
But it comes with destruction.
No one need that heat
Just you prey in the depth of the luscious movement
That's a signature signed by you.
He is quite greedy
And so are you too.

Cool child! reach,
Reach for the best
These games you're playing may cost you the rest.
Tap out a rhyme that creates a groan in your throat
that can attract the frightened beast.
Captured, satisfied, fulfilled, pleased,
Smile at your quest
You were made to be the best.

# *No More*

Grannie-Mitt had on pink
When she opened the door
We all got scared 'cause pink means
No more, no more.

Fighting, tolling and empty days working,
Loosing down on our knees.
Being beaten, defiled and alone
Gone, I've had enough, gone.

Grannie-Mitt kept singing
So soft, so, so sweet.
Seems as though the son/sun brightened up its
rays to color her beat.
She sang for old and included the new.
She sang for us now,
We heard the truth.
She sang all day, telling us what the Massa said.
She sang telling us what to do,
To stay out of harm's way.

To stay last days of cotton
No more tobacco
No children to work close to the shore

No more! No more!
Raping in front of our eyes
These days the river will open and close.
For you young ones to make a pose,
We cry in our souls
Because no tears can be seen.

One drop of water creates misery for a child
So mean.

Smile children as you work closer to freedom's train
God look down on us
And just bring the rain.
No more! No more!
Will my girl be defiled, ruined and casted out?
For her life has no value?
What you fretting about?
My girl child was beautiful, full of life and great knowledge
They all ruined her 'cause she spoke the word "college".

"College," she said, "I'm going someday."
Massa looked, "What did you say?"
He took out his time piece
And sent her to the trees
Pointed that way.
I'll be there in a while
Go sit on your knees.

I reached for him he pulled away,
"Granni-Mitt she's got to be taught
Shut that mouth
'Cause the others get ideas
From what she's talking about, school? college?
Then leading the world?
She gone crazy in that head of hers"
"Yes, Massa, yes, yes. I know.
Let Ma-ma have her. I'll save you a walk".

"I'll take that girl and we'll have her last talk
No more! Yes, no more"

"Give me the chain, the whip, and that blade,
when I'm done only God will know
What happen up under that tree-shade
No more, ever, no more, I say."

The tree planted near the water's edge just a quick way
to be washed right over the edge.
No more! Oh, no more!
As she floated away to freedom.

# Woman

Woman, oh woman
Where did you get that smile?
Creating a sunset when the world grows into its newness,
Look and feel as it crosses your face like the water of the Nile
Bringing warmth and love to the day
Woman, sweet woman
Where does that walk come from?
Does this music in your head transform the stride?
That make you glide
Like the ripples in the ocean
Moving with ease and grace?

Woman, dear woman
Is that somebody in your voice as does the breeze make
love to branches of each tree
Moving, dancing and caressing each leaf as it passes by
Woman, yes woman, where did it start?
Look back to your ancestors of old
Kings and Queens majestic and bold
Lessons were taught,
More priceless than gold.
She wrote the script
They were taught the lines.
Women play your parts,
Now the rest is mine.
Woman, oh woman.
Yes, women of old
Teach your daughters
For this was a test
It's your time to pass on the best.

# Hello You

Hello you,
Hello Sistah Friend,
Hi Sistah Woman,
Hey, hello, hi, Sistah Girl
Are we the same?
Sistah, us and them
Are we the salt of the earth?
Just a gem?
Is it our intent to trust?
Look at them,
See them in you and see you in them.
Hello people,
To see how you must feel,
To know where you begin and
I may end or continue.

Life's journey is a must,
We don't choose, it's given to us.
Rewind and think,
Did I live in that show?
What was my role?
When did the dress rehearsal start?
Did I miss the call again?
Will I get it before it ends?
Sistah, Woman.

Share your wisdom with me.
The universe creates a place for
our character to grow.

Plant your seed in my soil,
Let us fertilize the garden together.


I'm your interruption,
I'm here to show you your conscience.
Here is your game,
How long will it take to teach you the moves?
Will you be receptive and share?


Hello Sistah Woman,
Sistah Friend,
Look at me.
Don't you see when you look at
the great olive tree,
You see you and you see me.


Sistah Girl,
Strong, beautiful, timeless, sweet
Life happens, let's fix it,
Let's unite and live, love,
And let the unconditional favor of life fuel our happiness.
Know that the turtle found on the fence
Did not get there alone.
Sistah Friends
We are united
We are one.

# Just You Mama

Mama
My star of fate, destiny's child,
Mama.
My cushion,
A soft place to fall when the world
around me feels hard.
Mama guided my feet,
Tracing my steps
Bringing the love of wisdom
Connecting my soul to the destiny
of my existence.

Your strength molded me,
Your discipline guided me,
Your wisdom saved me,
I bow to you, Mama.
Listen, can you hear the wisdom
Through the quietness of her thoughts?
Can you stand to know how
effortless the wise woman speaks
to her destiny and yours?
Listen to the music that played in her soul,
You'll find the rhythm for you can
see the way she moves.
A worldly choir.
It connects us to the universe.
Rejoice. Renew. Listen.

# *Oh, Oh, Wow!*

Oh, it's just me,
I'm living for free.
I'm living in a house with a man I can't stand
And he proves, he can't stand me.
Ha ha! Just living for free
Stealing shelter, stealing food, eating
When he's gone, doing everything I could.
Just break the "mode"
Get off that slimy log.
The toad did!
He jumped off and swam away
into the clean water from the bog.

Yeah, it just hit me!
I'm living a complete lie,
Not half lie, not a third of a lie
A complete whole lie.
Others walk pass and say
"Boy would I kill to have a man like
that,
A life like that,"
Things like that.
And she says "Be truly careful of
what you wish for,
Because, Lord, I'm living for free,
In a space with the 'other'
that has set out to prove they can't
stand me."

It just hit me,
It woke me up out of my sleep,
I'm living the life of "Riley" it said.

*E. Pat White*

Inside this place with a creep.

I listened to the threats
And the silent conversation of pains.
Watching the face of the enemy and
what have the "other" gains.

I'm living for free.
In a cage of stench
Smelling of old love
that feeds the soul covering under a
blanket made with fibers of love.
Knotted with lustful mornings,
Passionate middays of kisses of fire
unending,
Evenings of whispers of sweet nothings that moves
through our bones.

Yeah. It just hit me.
I woke up from my sleep to find a big red vest.
The one I vowed not to buy.
Where am I?
On a journey called life
standing near yesterday.
Hoping tomorrow will come quickly
so I won't stray.
But, I'm living for free in a space
called home.
The "other" remains here but don't want to.
This cage is open

Why won't the "other" go
Because they are often a no-show
He's been living here for free.

Whose plan will work?
Whose plan will do?
Or will the war continue
Because he doesn't think
I know what's been done?
Yeah. It is living free.
In this space that's rooted like the olive tree.

# Brown Chic

Brown Chic.
Where did you come from?
We know that the black cow eats
green grass and rests on brown hay
and gives us "white" milk!
Aah. Then, where does your story begin?
Tell us your story.
What is it?

Oh, so did a cream-puff gent
rooster make love
To a dark- skinned woman (hen)
And produced a brown skin chic?
Is that your beginning?
Is it is, or is it ain't?
Tell me. Don't you know?
Brown-chic where lies your origin?
Were you created to bask in sin?
Causing a fuss just like girls do,
When? How? If?

Getting attention anyway you can,
Brown Chic take your stand,
Brown Chic trace your destiny,
Find your power within you.

Knowing from whence you came
is no sin,

Read, research and study some more.
Don't settle for any B.S.
Yes, B.S. I said so,
'Cause I've lived the game,
For I am a Brown Chic too.

A beautiful creation from the
hands of the only Potter,
That breathe life into nothingness.
No! Yes! Maybe!
Surely Nothingness.

Out steps a Brown Chic,
As sweet as morning dew,
As light as a butterfly's kiss,
As luminous as a sunset,
As beautiful as a gem,
As awesome as God's breath,
As precious as life.

Brown Chic! It's your time!
Stand up!
Applaud your existence.
Brown Chic.
That's us.
That's me.

# Done Told You

Mama done told you once,
Daddy done told you twice.
Why are you so hard-headed?
Not acting nice.
You stay in trouble with no free time in sight,
Ahh, trying to be good with all your might.

Mama misses nothing, she knows it all,
She even found out when you wore her heels
To make yourself tall.
Boy, don't you get it at all.
We done told you once trying to save your hide,
But your brain doesn't process right,
Nothing's on your side.
You keep looking for something to do,
Pulling us in to be your bad posse
And we did it too.

Wake up and smell the fresh air
For the roses are too sweet
'Cause when Mama gets your behind again,
You'll say that she wasn't fair
She just wanted someone to beat.

Daddy done told you that his wife doesn't play
So, listen to her orders and just do what she says.

Don't ever think you're smarter 'cause it won't work,
She'll figure it out and there comes the shout!
Boy, what are you up to on this day?
I've heard you're up to something on this day

I heard you screaming before your head went out the door.
Sometimes I think you think I'm crazy and such,
Not as smart as you and can't be touched.

Child you must be joking,
Poking fun at me and all.
I've been here longer and life
has taught me much
Gave me sense that I can make changes from.
So, slow your roll
Listen and learn,
Feel my touch,
Whatsoever you choose.
I see that smirk
That sinister look.
Hands in your pocket
Hiding something you done took.
I saw when you did it
while I was looking through my book.

Boy, come by me,
Make ace and more.
This ain't no game.
You're messing up my groove,
We done told you life maybe a game.

But the rules for you just ain't the same.
Mama told you once
Daddy said it twice
Nobody will wonder when you're caught
And there's a fine.

E. Pat White

# My Ride

Thunderbird! yeah, what can you say?
Got to get back to "kaki-laki"
Where life is laid back and sweet,
Where the living is cool and can't be-beat.
Girl, just styling, looking good and tight.
What? Watching the body language of those looking on.
They are intimidated just because I came home,
Coming back to "kaki-laki".

Styling, profiling, and sleek
Smiling at the night sky as the stars blanket the earth
Top down, music playing, wind on my face,
T-birds rolling, pointed toward our place.
The compound is ready, waiting to be enjoyed.
I'm sitting in the best,
Waiting to see the rest,
Knowing there will be questions
I must pass this quest.

Three hundred and fifty horse power is purring and free,
V8 engine, Bose audio-system
talking to me like an old friend,
One chapter has ended and the next always begins.

There have been a few bends in my fender
Because life hasn't been so kind,
But I keep going because this time is mine.
Being mean is a cover for life is sometimes so hard living
A lie can make breathing tough,
Each day can be a treasure.

Once we look forward to each day
Exhaling to release burdens.
God, who is in control?
Yes, I need some freedom
Just some old country air.
Daddy use to say
"Let's stand on the ditch-bank and stare".

Oh, life is awesome and I treasure every second
Getting it right brings it all together in sight.
Be happy because it lasts only for a while,
My ride was necessary to put me back on track.
T-bird, so smooth, what can you say?
Yours.
Mine.
Ours.
That's what living makes us see,
When you grow out of the "me",
It easily becomes "we".

*E. Pat White*

# *Up*

I'm up looking,
Just looking to see
what's outside of my window,
Past where the breeze is sweet to me.
I'm up.
Life begins to emerge and seek,
Looking for food,
Loving for fulfillment from
someone's love.
Aah, I say as life has again granted to me
God said "Y0es" and my new day
began
Thank you.
Yes, thank you.

Smiling I pray to my own self,
Felt good because this is a black
canvas to start a new.
Paint it with harmlessness, good
deeds and attitude,
Paint it with joy and pure gratitude.

Life is given because of the
"Master's Love",
Another chance at something to
prove your faith.
Commit, rejoice to something,
Be true,  pleasing everybody is overrated,

They came in groves looking to find your weakness,
So, you are baited.

Be a giver and feel how your heart laughs with joy
Big heart of colors,
Oh, it feels good, oh boy.

Be a child of the universe
Visible and free,
God's given me a new day
Just to praise and be me.
Shake the chain of the world off
and run like a runaway slave
Unshackled and free.

# *From Up There*

From up there
He can see forever.
Always, forever,
From up there he sees me, you, and them.
From up there all the colors sing a
symphony of melodies of unity.
From up there he sees them, too,
the melody, the song.
The hearts that are wounded, sore,
and hardened
He sees from up there.

The sky goes on indefinitely
Clouds so white, universe so blue
and a hue of love
just like a balding dove.
From up there everything is beautiful,
The wind feels sweet
The rain smiles as it falls
The sun says 'yes, it's great' from up there.

Who needs that and some of this?
Who needs those?
No, not you, not from up there,
From up there his eyes are ever open
His arms, ever waiting
His desires, ever present
His patience, ever patient,
His voice, ever soothing.

From up there life is serene,
Simple and nourishing
Never living for yesterday
or afraid of tomorrow.
Looking forward and living in the moment,
Just as it should be from down here,
Because from up there life is what it is.
His love in motion.
From everywhere.
From up there.

Wow! He's up there where the air stays sweet
Basking in a love that we could not meet.
Smiling, laughing, and greeting as he passes by
Knowing my wants will never be dim.
He loves us longer than anyone can
Now, he is dressed for God's heavenly band.
Singing, singing, singing.
Up there. Yes. Up there.

# Flight

Where's your imagination?
Where does it take you?
What is your dream?
You should have plotted a
direction it would seem.

Do you dream in colors?
Or again maybe just the fall.
Or do you feel lost in the "fight"
Of your destiny's call?

Where's your imagination?
It should lay out a plan,
Directing your ancestry
A foundation under "HIS" hand.
Think. Yes, think and take a stand,
Reach into yourself for direction and purpose.

Look at the eagle,
See its graceful flight
Following a cycle
That is guided by its keen sight.
High boundless never misguided or loss.
Always searching.

Look to be a flight of fantasy.
A diagram for you and me.
Dream with a goal,
Pray often and cleanse your soul.

Remember the journey,
Sharing with others
what's been told.
Realizing the purpose of growing old.

For your fight is now your connection with the universe.
Stay focused.
Say "how"?

# A Fool?

A fool? Yes, a fool I've already been
A fool, I've already dragged my feet,
Living someone else's life,
Their blueprint, very neat.
Not knowing the essence of what's me,
Just existing in a shell longing to be.

Wake up, breath, jump start your life,
It's your turn,
Begin, enjoy.
It's your life,
Take a breather, smile, relax
Your time, you're fine.

A fool no more,
Just enjoying what's mine,
Saying thank you to my destiny,
My life now is fine.
I will now live truly on purpose
Chasing my destiny, my fate.
Wow! It feels great.

When I was "a fool"
I didn't know myself.
Hidden, lost, no identity to speak.
Now I feel alive!
Live in joy!
Not feeling at all weak.

# Rise Up

Rise up my brother,
Take the bait
Care for your family
Truly that's your fate.
God gave you a "blueprint" to guide your way,
Read the "script" to direct your day.

Quiet your soul and be of good cheer
Look for your strength
It's your armor to wear.
Do your best and know who you are
Resign to be confident
God will do the rest.

Here lies your destiny in care and generosity,
Be a servant
Disciplined in the Word.
Listening to our ancestors
The way is truly clear.
Listen, speak, do
The journey is ours,
With us the burden never fare.

Yes, rise up my brother,
Take care of your soul,
Watch and wait
Do what you are told.
Rise up and walk,
The road is there
Just step out on faith and be bold.

That's the dare.

So, brothers, fathers, sons, uncles, and friends
Rise up.
Meet the challenge
Guide your family, with leadership and praise
Show the world just how you were raised.
Rise up!
Yes. Raise the torch of humanity,
Rise up!

# Me. Yes Me.

The black woman,
Yes, that's me!
So strong, so loving, just made to be.
Ask the mountain so vast and wide,
Equate its sight to the black woman's glide.
Smooth and sweet.
No time to waste, sipping on life just an awesome taste,
Ask her ancestors whose existence is her's
Beauty and brain that drives her fame,
Ask her lover who makes her whole,
Enjoying a lover's pleasure that's shared and not told.
Ask the universe that grew from her seed
Just ask and the answer fills a need.
Then ask the others who wish they were she
The one you speak of.

Yes, just me.
Me, the black woman with many miles to go.
Ask the moon that mirrors the sun,
I'm telling you so,
"I am" gave us pleasure to live – be - praise and have fun.
Forget the pain, the hardship and lost.
Look up to the heavens, just rejoice.

Glory! She's beautiful.
Yes, beautiful in and out,
Made by His blueprint without a doubt,
Be happy, be thankful,
Be just you, not me.
For I am the black woman
Just free to be me.

# A Heart

A heart is broken every day,
Giving love means you have to pay.
You give yours,
He walks away.
Only getting hurt on another day,
As he strays saying we are strong,
Pitches our feelings as the farmer does his hay.

Give trust, show peace and watch your faith grow,
For brokenness means there is always a lesson learned.
Hearts are broken
Just like yours and mine,
It happens in this world all the time.
So let's forgive and put the hurt aside
Listen to that same heart where all love abides.

Yes, rest that hurt upon the shelf
And just remember to protect you.
Be cautious, fair, and show that you care
Then love hard if you dare.
Right hearts are broken,
Just look around,
You'll see it too,
Watch the eyes,
The lesson is clear,
I'm one and so are you.
Broken by stress
We say don't exist
We cover the pain
By showing someone else's bliss.
I have hidden my heart

In a private place.
Protected from the old dust that can like lace,
Covering and squeezing the life from joy's space,
Holding me hostage without a trace.
Yes, a heart is broken
But love is our true destiny in this journey called life.
Alone, not lonely
Hurt, not broken
Lost, but never forgotten
As we live in love, with love, about love,
We will always mend in that secret place.
I did.

# *If*

If I could color the rainbow,
I'd color it bright and bold,
With hues of your smile that circle
my heart
Like gleaming pieces of gold.
If I could take that picture showing
the true being of you,
I would have to catch the wind,
For on it brings peace to my soul.

# *Lost*

She sits and weeps,
Her heart holds a secret.
She walks and looks,
Her existence bonds with the
newness of the day.
She sees.
She cries inside,
She knows, why. Why?
Yet, her heart feels it is lost,
It's her secret,
But everybody knows.

# Life Happens

Know that life happens with your input,
Ground yourself in the here and now,
Yesterday truly is gone, learn from it
Because you can't go back and do it over,
And tomorrow yes, tomorrow is a promise
Just, HOPE you'll be here when it comes.

# So Do I

Just as the sunflower bathes itself in the golden sunshine,
Raising its face to drink of the energy of life.
So do I.
Just as the tall oak tree raises its branches
to send praises to heaven on high.
So do I.
Just as a child reaches out to receive that
unconditional love and smiles.
So do I.
I am a child of the universe,
Forced to be in the game.
Righting the wrongs and holding my place.
So are you.
Just as I value the place where faith takes you to,
Long for the completion of your existence.
So do we.

*E. Pat White*

# *My Captain*

My captain loves me,
Just the way I am.
He sails with my rhythm on
peaceful waters
He smiles as the water brings forth
a challenge.
He walks with my stride,
Keeping the beat of my tune,
Humming along the song that
plays out in my head.

Yes, my captain loves me,
For he is me and I am him.

My captain loves me,
For we are one in this unity thing.
Unity that tells our hearts to sing.

My captain loves me,
Just the way I am.
His eyes caress my soul and rock it
back and forth like the motion of a
rip-tide on the sea.
His presence covers my being like
the warm blanket of the sky.

My captain loves me,
He wraps around the world
covering our existence with love,
pure, love.

My captain loves me
Just the way I am.
He cares about the boundless high,
Uniting our way with unconditional love,
as the wind tickles the branches of
the great olive tree.
His love tickles, yes, tickles me.

His love eases my pressure,
Like the stars in the midnight sky.
Softness, sweetness, brassiness, strength.

My captain loves me
Just the way I am.

# *Over Again*

Our heart grows with love,
Over again, yes, over again.
Love spreads and life starts all over
again.
Love starts in the twilight and the
atmosphere sets the mood.
Listen to the sweet music of the
robin's song,
A melody carried on the wind
Telling us what is soft, sweet and
lasting, yes, lasting.
And only when the heart grows and
love spreads and life starts.
Yes, life starts all over, again.
Over and over and over
Yes, over again.

# A Reflection

Moon beams dancing on the midnight lake,
Watch them move and sparkle and grace the night.
There go the souls of our ancestors
Mixing the tides.
Moving.
Sharing.
And holding on.
Look!
They stroll left and right,
Such beautiful grace to behold,
Colors, colors, colors.
Close your eyes and drink up the quiet,
Feel the perfect state of it all,
Just moonbeams.
They walk, trickle, and dance
in our hearts.
For they link us with the moving destiny of time.
See them in the rain,
See them in the rays of the sun,
See them in the hues of the rainbow.
Watch them form families in the night sky.
A reflection, illusion.
Hold on.
See the reflection of our soul.

E. Pat White

# Jen-A-Faye's Find

Yes. Jen-A-Fay found a penny,
That was all she had.
Didn't want to spend it
Because there could be no change
And she would be sad.

Just a little shiny cent that she found
Just lying on the ground.
Holding it up to the sun
as she turned round and round.
What will it get me if I go to the store?
Would it get what she really wanted
Some change to come back for more?

Oh, this penny, just a single cent,
Brought so many decisions.
Just money, but could make a dent.
Should I save it and look for more?
Sure, someone else dropped
another down by Johnny-Johnson's store.
Who walked by and dropped it?
To hurried to realize
Did not value its worth or its size?
Oh,this penny could be a life changing thing
That's what we often hear.

# Give Me the Money

They sing,
Decisions, decisions, they must be made,
For I can't spend my day wandering out
here in the shade,
People will pass by and look at me because
funny.
Then they might guess,
Oh, she has that money
Just a penny,
A small little "cent"
Maybe I'll just keep it and enjoy what I've found
when I get time to sit.

# *Life*

In the storm of life,
You call me by my name.
With a strong love that always
remains the same.
Just as you remain the source of
my strength,
I can carry on because life is my gift.
Who is the force that carries?
Is it "I am?"
Am I a part of this life?

# Something We Treasure

Oh! What is it,
Or what can it be?
Something we treasure so cautiously.
Ladies, did you hear me?
What can it be?
So wild, so calm, so laid back and free?

Listen!
You feel it in your heart,
Protect it in your soul.
We all need it as we grow old.
So, do you dare be remarkable
as the queens we all are.
Look at your reflections
to see who you are.
What is it?
Do you see?
Love, commitment, compassion and joy.
Take care of you so others can see.
What is it?
Integrity!

# *Butterflies*

Where do the butterflies go when
it rains?
The birds, the grasshoppers, too?
Do they dance in the water and
just do the same or make it
a game?
Where do they play?
As the water consumes the air
Do they try to hide?
And just count the raindrops the
way I tried

Oh, how beautiful and peaceful it
is here.
They fly by
Focused and quiet
So free – uninhibited -like me.

I just wonder where you go.
Do you know?
Living at peace is a treasure to
behold
For your eyes smile,
Your heart sings with wealth
untold.
Reach into yourself
And find your butterfly as the
answer lies at our feet.
Where do you go when it rains?

# *Friend*

Yes, a friend as precious as can be,
One who is dedicated and will
stand by me.
Finds the time to listen to my soul,
Helping me grow, forgives and
makes me whole.
She comes in and sits
and takes up little space,
Watching and praying
Knowing I need a face.
Pure, giving, doing and fair
Building us up…just knowing she cares.

A friend comes in and has par for the course,
Feeding your needs with what you need most.
A hug, a song, a head on her breast
Unconditional love is always the best.

A friend stands with us when others turn their backs.
Realizing we all sometimes get off the track.
Moving us back to reality,
That's truly the face of trust.

Friendships built on so many important things
Giving and receiving which makes our hearts sing.
Laughing, talking, and sharing of ourselves.
Spending quality time.
Lord, it's just the best.

When hardships come and we are lost in the storm,

Looking for comfort and sometimes finding none.
A friend steps in and finds what we need,
Always willing to nurture the positive seed.


Be true to yourself and be who you are
And watch how your essence can travel to the stars.
Just know in this life there is and will never be
Anything better than a Friend.


## *Covered*


If the storm gets rough again,
Come look for me.

Don't wade alone.
Come look for me,
Let's wade together.

Remember we are walking in His
mighty presence.

Yes, look for me.
He's yours, mine and ours.
Truly look for me.
I'm truly covered.
If I am, so are you.

# *When*

When do I start saying "No"?
When do I look away knowing?
When do I say "pass it on"?
When do I relax?
Just me, myself and I?
When do I just live my life?

My life with love and peace is abounding?
When? When does it become my time - ever?
Watch the others take heed,
Showing a caring side to others
without calling or thinking my name.
Why?
Why do I care so much?
Do I ever get to say no?

# Mama Said

Mama said "child, don't be lazy
expecting life just to do you right.
Learn to be spontaneous
Be loving.
Be your own self.
Stand for right.
Be a servant.
Be cheerful."

"Life is a great gift that will take
lots of challenges and work.
So work smart.
Do smile.
Never give up.
Stand with pride.
Stay positive.
Have fun.
Sing and dance."

"Quitting? Child, is that what I heard?
Quitting is not an option.
So find the time,
To pray.
To share.
To play.
To medicate.
To sacrifice.
To imagine.
To dream."

"Remember you are a part of the
"Walk-Away Society".
God has given us the night to rest
So our ability to labor is refueled
by the morning.
So my child our greatest fight
will always be the one we have
with ourselves".

"Our shadow is our shame,
Our defeats are a building place for
new experiences and wonder.
Then Recall, Relax, Rebuild,
Regain, Renew, Rejoice Restore,
And work with all but be labeled by none.

"Remain your own person,
Stay grounded in your faith.
Wear your protection everyday
Upright as we old folk say."

"Walking by faith and little sight,
Helps us keep the focus and keeps things right.
So Repent, Release, Relent, Relive,
Rebuild, Restore,
And know that your faith is the
inspiration for growth, child".

Mama said.
Yes. Mama said.

# *Quiet*

Come play with me
in the quiet waters of the sea.
Dance in the waves
as the current sings a sweet melody.
It sings to our hearts a song so soft and sweet.
A symphony of lines that just can't be beat.
Watch as the ripples move in the light,
Shudder but strong, with delight, yes, sweet delight.

Come play with me in the quiet waves,
Using your faith to stay afloat and be saved.
He knows our heart because He created it to be,
It beats to sustain life in you and me.

Come, yes, come.
Relax, enjoy with me in the quiet waves,
A place where this love truly saves.

# *Liberated*

Our light is what they fear,
Know that I'm powerful beyond measure.
I'm relentless and strong.
Look into my eyes,
They are the windows to see my soul.
See that light,
It was created in the image of God,
By God, for God Himself,
For His unending pleasure.

Look at your brothers,
Look at your sisters,
Look at them with that light,
See the beauty that has made you strong.
Faith is beauty.
Loyalty is beautiful.
Tenacity is awesome.
Drive your passion with unconditional love,
God's love.
It truly makes you great.
Yes, yes, notice us.
For I do - liberated.

Learn from the journey.
Focus on the destination,
Give life a chance,
Listen to the music.
It is what I dance to.
"The melody is smooth", said *Bob Marley*
The lyrics are tight,
The moves are slow and graceful.

Yes, the goal - focus and directed.
Get up, stand up, truly stand up for your rights,
Our rights, their rights,
Always take the high road.

Follow the eagle,
See it soar so high
High and free
just like you and me,
Rising in flight,
Giving all its might.
Liberated, educated, hopeful
because God made us that way
To continue to work hard today.

Listen to the melody in your heart
Know what it says:
Liberating, Liberated, and Free.

# When the Heart Waits

When the heart waits
the band renews it focus,
Locks its fears away
and looks forward toward tomorrow.

When the heart waits
love becomes sweeter.
Mornings become brighter,
Evenings reassuring,
Nights bearable as joy
awaits the dawn.

When the heart waits
A feeling of accomplishments surfaces,
A relaxed feeling of peace.
Each day shows a canvas
for a new painting of self.

When the heart waits,
Our purpose is driven by love.
Our confidence is built,
Courage becomes our friend,
Understanding floats like a soothing stream.

When the heart waits
just exhale and feel.
When the heart waits
love grows stronger.
It covers the sky
with a hue of beautiful colors
to warm our existence.

When the heart waits,
Humanity births
a new seed that gives to the world a child of
liberty and self-worth.

When the heart waits,
it prolongs the date that is in our future.
Hard to reach,
But moves closer day by day.

When the heart waits,
Just exhale and wait too.

## *Big Brother Speaks*

Big brother said we've got to go to the field,
Because there's cotton to be picked,
Big Jim's at the market you see.
Get on up and make daddy proud,
Stay quiet as you dress,
Shh!
Don't be so loud,
Hope he'll sleep till we get back,
'Cause I know he's tired of pulling that big old sack.
Fifty pounds, 100 pounds, 200 and four,
Pick that today and tomorrow Big Jim will want more.

There're their kids always wanting to play,
Yes, we do too, but we must put fun aside.
'Cause there's always something to do.
Big Brother said, "wrap it up to your own self nose,
For it's so cold, your eyes are running like a water hose".

Hurry, let's go girl rush,
Why are you so slow?
I know what you're thinking,
No hiding behind the door,
No school for you or any of us today
so walk lively and don't you stray.

Do your share
as the dawn will soon come
bringing us some light.
For we'll have to work again till night.

Night or day
Dark or light
Work smart, not hard with all your might.

We all have three jobs,
Like the farmers we are bold
rushing for the finish line
like Mama once told.

Yahoo, we heard her call.
Running toward the voice trying not to fall.
Kids that were so smart,
You all did more than your part.

Daddy will be more than happy
as he wasn't himself today,
But you made up for the pounds,
Sure, we will get the pay.

Let's meet at the china-berry tree,
Relax and play
For tomorrow will be
just another workday.

# *Awareness*

Today I found a gift,
The gift of quiet in my father's house,
Sat and watched the sun from the window,
As it took shape in the sky.
On so many different mornings,
It demanded presence and took it with quiet and ease.

I listened to a crow as it "kar" to be heard,
The gift of quiet can bring a great peace
And inner enjoyment of silence.

I listened as my heart moaned with a rhythm
In tune with that of the universe.
I saw, I felt, I loved.
A scurrying squirrel moving over the branches of time.
Soundless. Fearless and safe.

I sat and looked and listened,
The quiet of my inner self,
Soft, quiet, fearless, safe.
I had only to ask to be calmed and ease the rushing pace.
Slow me down so
I too can be a good listener
to my own destiny.

The sky brings a longing for boundless expectations,
On this journey we know as life.
My parents rest in solitude
As it is well with the world.

The unknown brings a longing and excitement each day,

My daddy smiles with unconditional pleasure
as a new day dawns his journey today.
Yes, pleasure on Mama's face

As the duty to please sets like rivers.
Her movement - few things in this life moves as consistently as time.
For it's smooth and easy continuously truly divine.
Never ceasing to stop for a second,
Truly that's time!
Smelling the nurturing food
that strengthens and fuels our existence.
Just as the Word fuels our souls
For such times as these.

# Growing Wise, Not Old

Old, did you say old?
Yes, I'm old by the standards of my birth,
But not my heart.

But knowing how I've lived,
Proves that statement wrong and such.
Reaching this age comes from having self-worth and
still a song.
Yes, I sit for hours on end
here in my favorite chair,
Like it's my old friend
dawning his old sock
as neatly as I can.

True, I walk very carefully with my helper Ben
Which I named my cane.
Aah, in the eyes of the universe I'm labelled wise,
But somehow unless 'cause I'm in the way of society,
Always making a mess.

I sit here in peace enjoying the memories of yesterdays,
Watching, comparing, enjoying, if I dare.
The coolness of each evening makes it a must,
Covering my shoulders with a shawl,
Helps building trust.

Yes, sitting here by the window
where the breeze tickles my face,
Bringing pleasure from a faraway place.
In the quiet of the daybreak
my solemn heart sooth from pain,

By thought of a love that was and gone again.
Now I sit nod, recall, relax and exhale,
Feeling the time as it escapes my reach.

Learning to live and love unconditionally
was what "Ma" and "Pa" preached.
Old, child my sight may have gone dim,
But in my heart, I still know all of them.
Know that what's planted in our hearts never grows old.
It keeps the memory young.

Yes, my moves are calculated, my reach carefully done.
Don't want to fall 'cause that would be no fun.
People don't really want to help unless you're the
favorite one.
Now, I laugh 'cause life's a blast,
Everyday building a foundation of strength that
hopefully will last.

Power comes with wittiness, courage and understanding.
I stay focused on my goals
'cause you never know where you are landing.
Do good.
Be good.
Speak well of others.
Yes, we are the keeper of our brothers,
Age is more than a number
just as priceless as the stars.

The years have slowed my roll,
Not my spirit or worth.
My head is bowed not in shame,
But constant prayer to Him who holds my name.
I sing to the distant symphony of all that I will be.

I'm old, they say, but know God has not discarded me.
Things have changed they say but who are they?
This age thing is happening to you, up to this day.
Age is wisdom and wisdom does come with time
I'm glad to enjoy for to the entire world is a stage of mine.

Yes.
Old.
Fine.
Fresh.
Guarded.
And fit.

Age is what you find when God is by your side,
As you sit now when you're feeling so old
and don't like how you look.
Think of the Creator and the time it took,
Forming a you with such a soul,
You must be awesome,
I'm told age will come,
Just keep living and you will see.
So my Mama with the faith from within told me.

# My Sistah

My sistah where are you?
Call! Come. Sit.
Yes, sit with me.
We can smile, laugh, hug, cry,
share and try to mend the hurt.
Come and let's walk this road together,
Share your feelings in a way,
Feminine kind of way.
Have to, for tomorrow is just a breath away.
Be tender.
Be confident.
Be open.
Be frank.
Be safe.
Come with me and just be.
Yes, frighten may not be so bad at times,

Sistah, let's bridge that gap of loneliness
So come.
Call.
Sit.
Smile.
Hug.
Share.
And just be.

# *So Satisfied*

Won't be abused.
Won't be misused.
If necessary, I'll choose.

Can't walk out of my door to lose,
So satisfied, just satisfied
Not settling.

Not just getting by
Won't play this game.
To satisfied, just satisfied.

Got me a guide.
Follow the blueprint,
Not going alone for this ride.
Safe direction,
Covered with great protection
Satisfied, truly satisfied,

Mama said, "Know that life is full
of surprises.
If you live long enough, you'll see".
Daddy said, "Keep on living
and you'll find out where the
rough road leads."
So satisfied, be satisfied.

Don't walk around blindfolded
Not caring to see.
No.
Open up.

Be brave.
Live.
Life is truly fun,
Complicated but sweet.
Set a goal, plant a seed.
It's your life
You know what you need.
Gather your harvest,
Smile at your growth
Satisfied, Just satisfied.

## *Change*

Being kind is no shame,
Didn't you know
even seasons know when to change,
Showing us that nothing will remain the same.

Winter lends its space to the springtime,
Sets the framework for the summer.
Then the summer brings back the fall.
Brrr, I'll take my stand.
Let's start over again
So know that some changes are good.

## Slow Down

It happens in a flash.
In seconds that it takes to look back
at what you should have done.
It's too late.
No, it doesn't take long to watch our today
become yesterday and we become lost,
overwhelmed, burdened, heavy ladened.
Sad.

We all want to leave a legacy,
An offering that we don't have to apologize for.
Needing to be worthy of the life and space we enjoyed.
Seconds come like lightning as time continues to move,
Trying to hold onto the past, something to prove.
Slow down and enjoy.
Hopefully moving in the right directions,
Letting our experiences help to form our protections.
Don't we ever think that just being is a prayer in itself,
Learning to truly relax, relent, exhale, and slow down.

# *Big Mama's Guilt*

Yes child, now what did you say?
That's alright, daddy will get you today,
Get on the train half pass mid-night,
Just pray and ride,
You'll be alright.
Much too young to plot a trip to glory,
Fight those demons
You too have a story,

Bound for home to your southern roots,
Leaving behind the hurt and the worry.
What will Mama say when she hears what I did?
Maybe I won't say
I'd keep it hid.
My heart is heavy.
My tears are many.
I have no words
I don't have any.

We said, "I'm here," but where is here?
I looked around and no one's there,
My chest was burdened,
I screamed out loud.
The paper said, "He's gone."
I'd like to know where? How?

Mama, oh Mama
For such times as these.
I was found down on my knees.
Brother said "Go,

Eddie will know what to do
Because he has always taken care of you.
Call Granny-Mitt, she's got the advice for you.
We all have a skeleton in the closet, too."

"We'll be at the station,
You are never alone,
Big-Mama quilt awaits you.
A sin stoned.
Looking and loving,
No one to tell
He's gone now,
Nothing to share."

"Three days of rest will turn you around
Under the quilt
Cleansing can be found.
Close your eyes
Cry no more
Mama's got the remedy
It's been used before".

"Lay still my child,
The quilt carries a price.
Cover up good as I give the advice.
Get deep in your plac,
We sweat out the hurt.
Replacing your soul with unconditional trust."

"Give it to the Master
None of us can judge,
He wrote the book.

Talk to Him
That's all it takes.
There's a day for your Father.
The next for His Son,
Last for the Holy Ghost
The Trinity,
All in one."

# Delilah's Touch

She laid in lust.
He laid in love.
Gave his all in every thrust.
Loved and shared,
Thought she cared
So he gave it all again and again.
Relaxed and fell in her son.

She showed desire,
She set the tone
for she played the game using him as the pawn.

Act truly bold,
Get all you can,
Then get out fast
He'll be killed,
You still have had a blast.

Sick and sly,
Quick and evil she took.
He fell in like a baby
needing only her milk.

He gave.
She took and said "stay."
He smiled but did not see
when she smirked as it melted away.

I have all I need now.
My plan has worked.

*E. Pat White*

I know the secret.
I used my perks.

I'm lost, I'm broken, I'm vexed, and scared.
God, where are you? I'm all alone
With strength comes weakness
They travel as twins, you see.

Fill me, guide me
as I pray my strength in you this day.
Love is precious
and is made to be kind,
Not so much when you're not mine.

Treacherously driven,
Deceptive and crude,
She needs you weak to keep on living.
Longing, ambitious, determined and smooth,
A hidden agenda used to soothe.
Lusciously she moves into his sight drawing him in
So easily.
That's no sin.
Disarm and accessing the passionate moves,
Filling him with love to gain his trust.

She sees me.
She needs me.
She wants me.
Yes, so much.
Not knowing it will change after the first touch.

Determined to lead,
Giving it all she's got,
Pulling him in,

Only to be believed
she has a plot.

Lost in passion
A love for you and me we are hidden,
Thinking no one knows or sees.

Involved with a pro that led you on,
Looking upon her beauty that kept you stoned.
Delilah's touch was deadly and devious,
Too sinful and cozy,
Seeking to destroy, who?

# Understanding

I see.
Do you?
I was.
Were you?
I know.
Do you?
I received.
Did you?
I prayed.
Won't you?
I'm covered.
Are you?
I've prayed
Can you?
I've shared.
Will you?
I can do all things
through Christ who strengthens me. (Philippians 4:3)
Can you?
Delight yourself in the Lord and
He will give you the desires of your heart.
(Psalms 37:4)

# *Once Free*

I was once free like the Cherokees,
Moving through the universe like the eagles and bees.
Until the power that be
tried to take control of me.

My spirit still rides like the wind,
A flight so effortless, it is no sin.
High and fast, keeping all in sight,
Stretching and teaching with all my might.

Mama says not yet.
Daddy says when?
Falling down ain't bad,
Just work to get up again.
Stop reaching back.
Go forward.
There's happiness for you and me.

We were once free
Because life is just to "be"
Walk in peace
Show you are humble and things fall into place.
My spirit still ends fast and free.

Looking and feeling happy and with me
Giving to share,
Sharing to give.
I need this freedom
so I can live.

# *Mother*

Mother was created from the ribs in daddy's side,
She practiced her moves to glide with a sweet stride.
They united in love
A passion so true,
Building a family that included
you and me.

They walked in harmony from dawn to dusk
Finishing each other's sentences with faithful trust.

She read the Bible
Following the blueprint to the word,
He followed her lead
and sang to be heard.

The melody met
and joined in sweet love.
Creating the clan.
Yes, that's us.
They truly built trust.

She was blessed in grace,
Blessed in mercy, too.
Faith as you know always walked close,
As she looked to the hills

For God only knows,
She maintained the strength
that guided us through.
Making us strong and self-reliant,
Faith driven and true.

# Langston and Me

Our people, Langston says.
The night is beautiful
So are the faces of my people.
Langston says, The stars are beautiful
So are the eyes of my people.
Beautiful, also is the sun.
Beautiful, also are the souls of my people.

I say, The world is awesome,
So are the lives of our ancestors.
I say, Our hands are skillful,
So are the deeds of our families.

Langston says, Beautiful.
I say, Awesome.
He says, Eyes.
I say, Hands.
Awesome, we both say.

Is our faithfulness.
So is the destiny of our lives.

I say love.
I say passion.
I say life.

The world is truly beautiful and
so are we.
Langston says, walk slowly.
I say stand, give, love
and find time to understand the plan.

# *Daddy*

Daddy was born before the wind
Just a few flashes in front of the sun
Like the rays that will shine to the core of everyone.

Daddy was born before the wind,
Know that his life is (was) vast like running streams
Sweet and soft like the colorful moonbeams,
Oh so caring like a true love it seems.

Daddy was born before the wind
Daddy was a love child
In the days of old.
Moving through his life,
A true and guarded soul.
Living a life both simple and new,
Giving back to the universe seeds that are true,
Yeah, my daddy was born simple and new.

God loves a cheerful giver that we know is true love
It was and is handed down on the wings of a dove.
Daddy knew,
He heard it when the wind whispered and it blew,
You were before I came.

Yes, daddy was born before I came,
Just a few flashes in front of the sun
Like the rays that will shine to the core of everyone
Yes, daddy was born before the wind.

# *A Peaceful Place*

Hey, there's a couple that rocks on their porch,
Waves to all who passes by because they're happy in this place,
They ride real slow and the town folks know
there's no hurry 'cause there's not many places to go.
But they all know where the destination ends.

He handles the wheel like it is gold
And he's ten feet tall,
Just living the life and having a ball.
Pleasant Grove, it is called.
All three miles,
No more, no less.
One and all are pleasing like that.
A wave.
A smile.
A laugh.
Few cries.
No lies.
Just pleasant memories of days gone by.

People leave,
they also return with big smiles.
Leaving us with few good-byes.

Yea, they rock, they walk, and they
wave and talk,
Slowly, we get it too.

A peaceful place is found out here,
We love to be there.

# Southern Life

Cool mornings, wet dew,
Hot coffee, cocoa or sweet tea black, light and
sweet, yea.
Tales set so daintily and neat
treats in small dishes.
Waiting to serve little feet,
Southern life that's sweet.
A smile from Mama,
Confirming the heart,
Knowing her baking can't be beat.

Chores to be done from dawn to dust.
No one escapes work,
Do your part,
It's based on trust.
Southern living, that's a must.

Oh, that hot sun!
So high, so bright.
Eyes covered over with hats
and caps to block the light.
Mama calls.
Daddy looks.
For he knows how long the midday break takes,

Time keeps moving without a hitch,
Soon we will end up near the ditch.
Just like "ole" mule moves with a destination ahead.
Work hard today to rest later in bed,
Tired hands, sore backs, weary souls and such,
Working smart, not hard will reward you much.

Sweet breeze.
Warm night.s
A squeeze.
A touch.
Sharing unconditional love
that's needed so much.

Mama looks
Daddy smiles
We giggle for we know
They love each other
Yes. We do, too.

Yes, cool mornings, cocoa and hot tea.
Hot coffee, just black or light and sweet,
Southern life for us was always
Days and nights of mama's treats.

# *Bright, the Soul Spot*

Right on this street,
Then left at the light move on over to the spot
called *Bright*.
Walk on in and you can sit right down,
Big Mable is waiting to woo you with her sound.
It's tender.
It's soft.
It's sweet.
It maybe what I need
Something to keep my
love-boy Pete.

Pete. Yea, he's so sweet.
A hard worker.
A provider.
A man of means.
Just a country boy.
Needing to be on the scene.

Cruise out this way so you can see
the place called *Bright*.
'Cause of the way it glows in the night.

Lay back
Close your eyes
Just feel the beat,
Be cool, no one's in a rush,
Take a seat if you trust.
Settle in and wait for the singer to sing.

What can I do for you?
The song and me.

So, enjoy, stay awhile, make yourself at home.
Know that travelers need somewhere to roam.
You took that right,
Left at the light.
Yes, right there at the corner,
Come on into the
*Brigh*t and do what you want.
No one will tell
Loneliness does sell.

# The Walk to Stand

Get outta here Bubba,
You know you can't drink there
or come in this door.
You better stop now
I ain't telling you no more.

Big "Ma-Mae" gave you life,
She wiped your tears,
She slept by you to quiet your fears,
Now you yell at her saying,
Get outta here,
Don't here, there or anywhere.
I'll go this time, but will come again,
To get my right 'cause I will walk to stand,
Yes. I know we all have a plan.

She sat on the porch of the old shanty-slave house,
Rocking and singing and
remembering, just remembering.
Yes, my dear we go today with playful hearts
and a vision we sort.
This ain't right, the old wise man said,
Again 'cause on that flag my families blood
made a stain.

You feed that baby from your fountain food,
Giving him life under all that pain.
They live with our strength,
Our bread of life,
Yet you ain't good enough,
Just ain't right mama, no

Not right at all.

Remember when "lil-Missy" came running down the lane?
'Cause he wouldn't eat for her the same,
Gave him to you to save their name,
No color, no race mattered then
Just Ma-Mae's breast was the best.

Today's the day that things will change,
That boy will help, they have to pay that debt.
I'm walking up to the front, no back door, no more.
Looking up with a smile in her eye,
She already knew he did try.

Sit and rest for there's much to do,
You must keep your head about you.
Then he touched her hand softly and said,
Been cooking, too.
I smell the love in that bread,
I'll have a piece to keep my strength up
'cause this fight ain't for a weak pup.

Then he said, "Are we walking again up to town?"
Walking together, hand in hand,
A force of change and yes,
Dignity plotted and planned.

Remembering the back doors,
Water fountains out of reach,
Back seats and cattle cars,
Through all these places our people met,
A journey through all this life is not easy to repeat.

# Lord, I've Got My Country Praise On

Straw in my teeth,
Shades on my eyes,
Feathers in my hand,
Glory over my head,
Grace in my plans,
Mercy covering my back,
Lots of promises in this cotton sac.

Jesus, the Son of man watching over me,
Even He knows this hard work can't you see,
Walking, singing and worshipping Him,
Yes, I've got my country praise on.

# *An Ode to Annie*

| | |
|---|---|
| **A** | Anointed and amazing |
| **N** | Nurturing and noble |
| **N** | Nourishing and noteworthy |
| **I** | Initiative and intelligent |
| **E** | Energetic and entrusting |
| | |
| **V** | Valuable and vivacious |
| **E** | Effectual and elaborate |
| **N** | Natural and neighborly |
| **I** | Interesting and inquisitive |
| **C** | Caring and cautious |
| **E** | Engaging and effective |

## AKA

## QueenAnne.com

www.ingramcontent.com/pod-product-compliance
Lightning Source LLC
Chambersburg PA
CBHW071128090426
42736CB00012B/2055